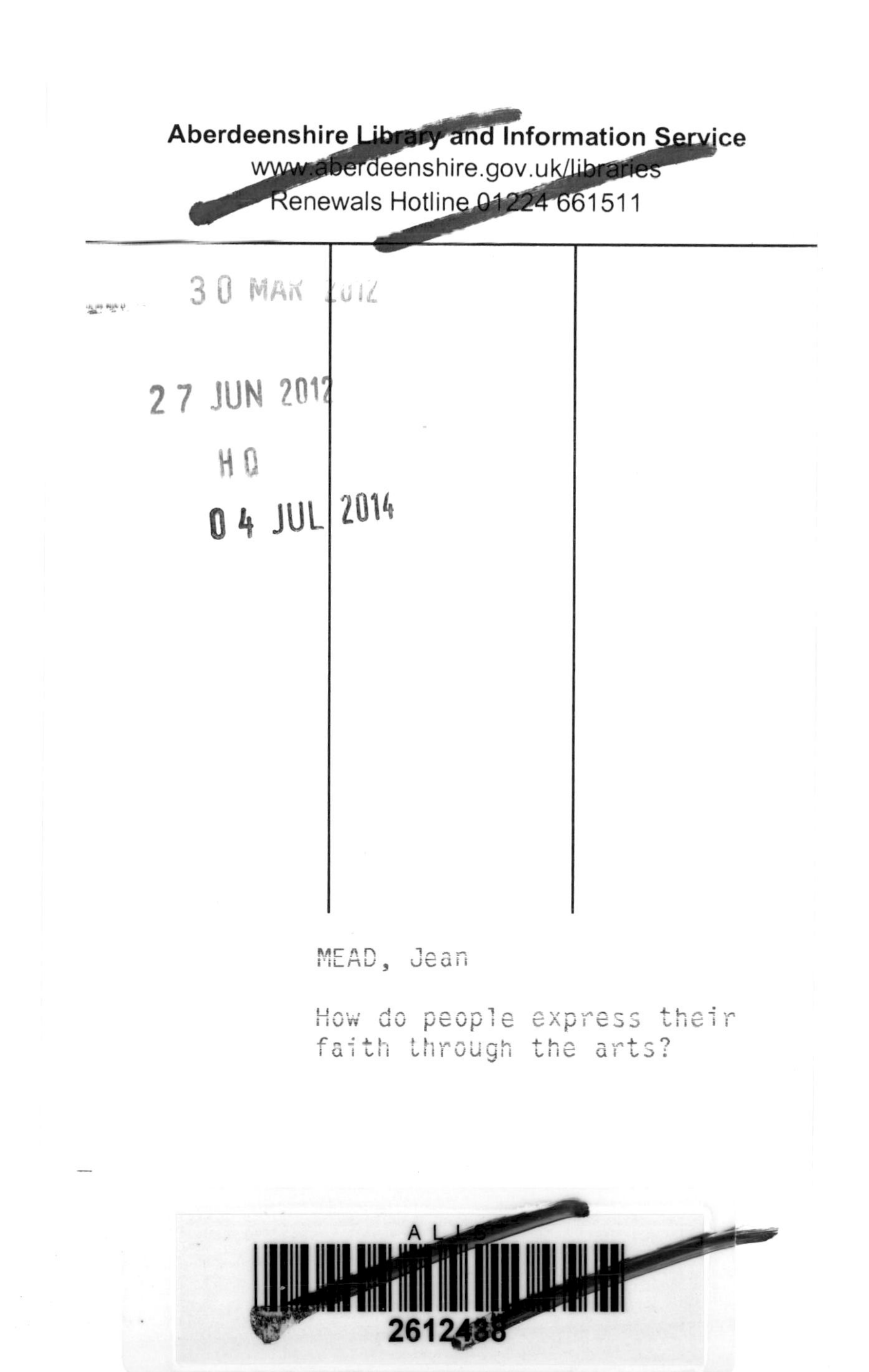
Aberdeenshire Library and Information Service
www.aberdeenshire.gov.uk/libraries
Renewals Hotline 01224 661511
30 MAR 2012
27 JUN 2012
HQ
04 JUL 2014
MEAD, Jean
How do people express their faith through the arts?
ALIS
2612488

STEP-UP
RELIGION

How do people express their faith through the arts?

Jean Mead and Ruth Nason

Published by Evans Brothers Limited
2A Portman Mansions
Chiltern Street
London W1U 6NR

Produced for Evans Brothers Limited by
White-Thomson Publishing Ltd,
Bridgewater Business Centre,
210 High Street,
Lewes, East Sussex BN7 2NH

Printed in China by New Era Printing Co. Ltd.

Design and illustration: Helen Nelson at Jet the Dog

British Library Cataloguing in Publication Data

Mead, Jean

How do people express their faith through the arts? - (Step-up religion)

1. Faith in art - Juvenile literature 2. Arts - Juvenile literature 3. Religions - Juvenile literature

I. Title II. Nason, Ruth

203.7

ISBN-13: 9780237534110

Acknowledgements

Many thanks are expressed to the following for their help in preparing this book: Tracey Lockwood, Sandra Walsh and children at Skyswood School, St Albans; Robert Cooper, Chris Foxton, Zarah Hussain, Ian Johnson, Gloria Stoney, Lana Young, the music group at Blackhorse Road Baptist Church, Walthamstow, the Bhavan Institute of Indian Dance and Culture.

Photographs are from: AFP/Getty Images: pages 5b, 21l; Alamy: pages 5t (The Photolibrary Wales), 17b (Hemis), 18b (David Sanger Photolibrary), 19b (Religious Stock), 23b (Duncan Hale-Sutton), 25bl (Huw Jones), 26t (ArkReligion.com); Bhavan Centre, London: cover grid br, page 25tl, 25tr; The British Library Board: page 10t, 10b; Robert Cooper: page 11t; Corbis: pages 7b (The Gallery Collection), 18t (The Art Archive), 20t (Arthur Thevenart); Chris Fairclough: cover tr, pages 4l, 4r, 15bl, 15bc, 15br, 26bl, 26br, 27 (all); Zarah Hussain: page 20b; Istockphoto: cover tl, pages 6c (Jennifer Fair), 6b (Carmen Martinez Banus), 12t (John Woodworth), 16l (Tetyana Kochneva), 24; Ian Johnson: page 19t; Kippa Matthews: page 23t; Jean Mead: cover grid bl, pages 8c, 8r, 9r, 16r, 21r, 25bc, 25br; Michael Nason: cover grid tc and tr, pages 6tr, 7t, 11bl, 12b, 13b, 14, 15t, 17t; National Trust Photo Library/David Sellman: page 13t; Rex Features/Paul Brown: page 9l; White-Thomson Picture Library: cover grid tl and bc, pages 8l, 11br, 22 (all Chris Fairclough).

Contents

How do people express their feelings? 4
Think about being creative 6
How do people use music in worship? 8
Creating beautiful books and texts 10
Cathedral building 12
Stained-glass windows 14
Different colours, different feelings 16
Picturing Jesus 18
Islamic art 20
Drama and plays telling Christian stories 22
Hindu art, dance and drama 24
Present a story through drama 26
Glossary 28
For teachers and parents 30
Index 32

How do people express their feelings?

Faces and body language

Can you tell what people are feeling, from the looks on their faces and from their 'body language'? Perhaps you have done some work on this in drama lessons.

▶ *You could experiment with drawing simple faces, keeping the mouth the same, but changing the eyes and eyebrows to show feelings such as anger, anxiety or surprise.*

We found that you can give faces different expressions by changing the shape of the eyes and eyebrows.

◀ *In groups, you could act out a situation, for others to guess the feelings you are expressing. Can you tell the feelings of each character in this scene, in which a famous footballer is spotted in the street?*

What postures and facial expressions would you use to express joy, love, pity, generosity, anger and jealousy?

Writing, pictures and music

Sometimes people express their feelings by writing a poem, making a picture, or playing some music. Do you sometimes hum, sing or move around to music when you feel especially happy? Which happy music do you choose?

▼ *In music, which feelings could you express through different rhythms of the drums?*

JOY

When you're on the next swimming level
Being invited to your friend's house
Passing my violin exam
Playing the piano.

The smell of chocolate melting in the sun
The sound of people not fighting in tag
The sound of wrapping paper being opened

A purple kind of colour
The sound of my cat going meow, meow, meow

Joy!

(Georgiana McCarthy)

▲ *Could you write a poem, like Georgiana's, about another type of feeling? Notice how she has thought about different senses.*

The arts

All types of creative work (for example, painting, sculpture, photography, writing, music, drama and dance) are known as 'the expressive arts'. This book will look at how the arts can help people to express their religious feelings and beliefs. What do you think are some 'religious feelings'?

◀ *For a Hindu artist, making pictures of the elephant-headed god Ganesh is a way of expressing devotion. You will find out more about Ganesh later in this book.*

Think about being creative

A very special thing about human beings is that they are creative. They make pictures, sculptures, music and stories, using all kinds of materials in inventive ways. They think it is important to try to make their creative work as good as possible. They hope that the art they create will touch people's feelings.

To create something, you use your observation, imagination and practical skills. Observing the shape of brazil nuts gave one artist the idea of making them into the bodies of some lively-looking model birds.

Why be creative?

People create art, music and stories for many different reasons. It may be for fun or to earn money or to give to someone. It may be for a special place, or to remember or celebrate a meaningful event. It may be to express an idea that they want other people to think about.

Do you sometimes make a picture for someone you love? People often say that this is the best type of present they receive.

After the end of the Second World War, an artist created this sculpture to be a reminder 'that human dignity and love will triumph over disaster and bring nations together in respect and peace.' The sculpture is called 'Reconciliation'. What feelings do you think it expresses?

Where does creativity come from?

Many people think that creativity is a very special, valuable human quality. Some people believe that God, the Creator of the world, inspires humans to be creative too. Creativity is a kind of energy that comes from God. What do you think?

People may feel that when they write or paint or do other creative things, this somehow continues God's creation. Some people use their creativity in particular to express their love for God and other religious feelings. Some examples are in this book.

The Italian artist Michelangelo (1475-1564) painted this idea of 'The Creation of Adam' on the ceiling of a church in Rome. It seems to show God's creative energy passing on to Adam, the first human being.

Favourite pieces of art

In class, talk about your favourite pictures and sculptures, and the feelings they seem to express. Do some of them remind people of good, positive things? Are some special because of who created them?

How do people use music in worship?

All kinds of feelings can be expressed in music. Which did you think of, on page 5? In several religions people sing to praise God, and some prayers are set to music. Some people use their musical talent to lead the singing or play instruments at services in their place of worship. People may feel that, in music, they are offering something beautiful to God.

▲ *Sikh musicians called ragees lead the singing at services in a gurdwara. Sikh hymns are verses from the holy book, the Guru Granth Sahib, and they are sung to tunes that were written by some of the ten Sikh Gurus. The ragees play instruments called the harmonium and tabla.*

Listen to some worship music

An interesting website to explore is www.request.org.uk. From the main site, click on 'Do what', then on 'Music', and you can see videos and listen to examples of music used by different groups of Christians when they worship together. When you listen, what feelings do you think are being expressed through the words and music? Do you find joy, reverence, wonder, thankfulness, humility? Do some people move to the music?

▼ *Gloria sings with the music group at her church. In Christian worship, some of the music and hymns are traditional, linking people now to worshippers in the past, but new hymns and modern music are used too.*

Music stirs something deep inside. It's a release, and I love singing the beautiful poetry from the Bible.

▲ *The choir at Westminster Cathedral sings for services, called Mass and Vespers, every day, and for festivals and concerts. The cathedral has a choir school, where the boys do ordinary lessons but also are trained to sing. Many cathedrals are well-known for their music, and many ordinary churches have choirs too. They often sing to the accompaniment of an organ, or sometimes a piano.*

The music sounds special and mysterious, and can lift my mind away from everyday things. It can make me feel that all is well.

Different opinions

What do you think is the effect of singing words to a tune or chanting them to a rhythm? You might say that it makes the words easier to remember, or that it helps people to speak the words in unison. A tune can express the feeling of the words and makes the words more special. On the other hand, you might say that sometimes it's impossible to hear the words that people are singing. Perhaps people become so used to chanting or singing words that they don't think about what they mean.

Religious people have mixed points of view like this. Some say that music helps people to concentrate on praying and praising God, or to experience and share the feeling of a religious festival. But there is a worry that people might be 'carried away', loving the music but forgetting God. To prevent this, some religions have rules that only the human voice or only some instruments may be used in worship. No music is used at all in most Muslim worship.

Festival music

In groups, compose some music or write a new song for a religious festival that you know about. What types of sounds will help to express the feeling of the festival?

Creating beautiful books and texts

Calligraphers and artists put special love and care into making copies of holy books, because they respect and treasure the words and teachings in the books. In several religions, people believe that the words in the holy book are words from God.

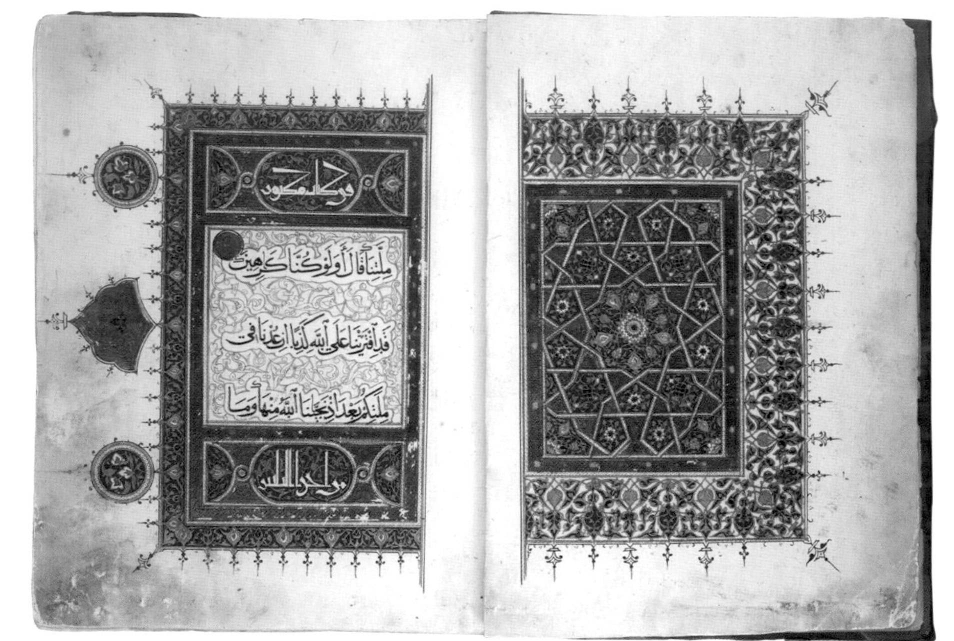

▲ *In this Qur'an the Arabic calligraphy is surrounded by intricate patterns. The right-hand page, full of pattern, is called a 'carpet page'. Muslims believe that the words in the Qur'an are God's message to all people, which was brought to them in Arabic by the Prophet Muhammad.*

Illustrations

Muslims and Jews do not use pictures of people or other living creatures in their holy books. They believe that to do so would break God's commandment not to make images. (You can look this up in Exodus 20: 4.) Most Christians do not interpret the commandment in that way, and so Christian Bibles may include pictures of people and animals.

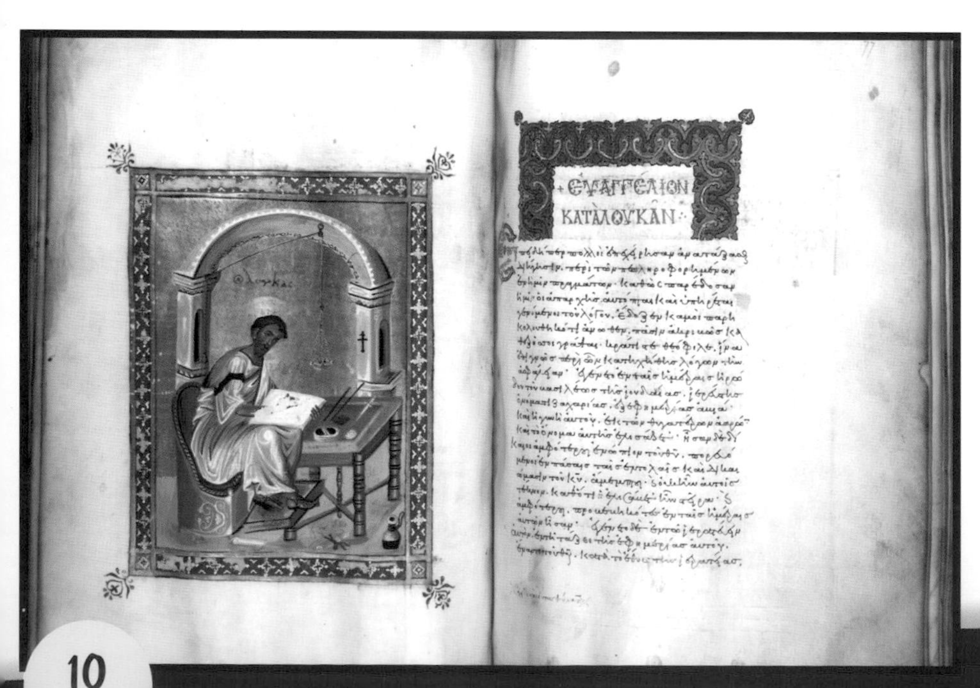

◀ *In the Middle Ages Christian monks made beautiful copies of the Bible, especially the New Testament. This is the beginning of the Gospel of Luke, in a New Testament written in Greek in the 10th century. The painting shows Luke writing the gospel. What effect does the gold colouring have?*

▲ *This calligraphy of a Christian prayer was created by Robert Cooper. On the right, he describes how the work came about.*

My craft is making beautiful writing. Jesus was also a craftsman: a carpenter. One day, after a tree had been cut down, I found a lump of wood. It reminded me of my favourite prayer, which describes how Jesus, even when he was dying on a wooden cross, was still working like a carpenter – though instead of crafting beautiful and useful things, he was crafting beautiful and useful people.

I didn't plan where to write the words of the prayer, but just looked carefully at the wood to see where to begin. As I wrote, with my small pointed brush, I saw there was not room for the words 'rough hewn' where I had made the wood smooth for writing. Then I realised that I could use the wood that was still rough as a background, to show what 'rough hewn' means: it describes what wood is like before the craftsman has sawn and planed and polished it. This made the calligraphy look more interesting too.

Artists call this sort of thing 'a happy accident'. To me, it felt more like receiving a gift, enabling me to express more clearly what the words mean.

Inspiring words

Passages from holy books and other religious writings often give artists ideas for their work. You could look for examples in pictures, on banners and on artefacts at any places of worship you visit.

◀ *Lana Young loves to do and teach embroidery. She is Jewish and sometimes makes mantles for Torah scrolls. A crown is a symbol of the Torah.*

▶ *For this mantle, she used the colour and flow of water, thinking of Isaiah 55: 1: 'All you who are thirsty, come to the water.'*

Your favourite text

A short saying from a holy book is sometimes called a 'text'. Choose a saying that is important to you, from a holy book, poem or other source. Design and make a poster with the saying as the focus.

Cathedral building

In many religions people build beautiful, impressive-looking places of worship. In Britain, where Christianity has been the main religion for hundreds of years, some of the finest examples are the cathedrals.

Sometimes people think of a place of worship as 'God's house', and this is one reason why they try to make the building as perfect as they can. When you make a picture for someone you love, you try to do your very best drawing and painting. In the same way, because people love God, they try to do their highest-quality work in building and decorating a place of worship.

People may also say that they wish their place of worship to be 'a witness to God' – in other words, to tell people about God. They hope that, outside and inside, the building will enable people to feel close to God.

▲ *Cathedrals, such as the one at St Albans (above), are important places of worship. They are also visited by many tourists, who go to admire the buildings and learn about their history.*

◀ *This stained-glass window in Lichfield Cathedral commemorates re-building work that was carried out after parts of the cathedral had been destroyed in the English Civil War. Can you see the plan of the cathedral?*

A tree cathedral

Many cathedrals were built in medieval times. Others are more modern buildings. In autumn 1930, Mr E. K. Blyth saw a cathedral that was being built in Liverpool and he was impressed by the beauty of its design and the skill of the stoneworkers. He explained what happened on his way home:

I saw the evening sun light up a coppice of trees on the side of a hill. It occurred to me then that here was something more beautiful still and the idea formed of building a cathedral with trees.

▲ *This is the nave, the main part, of the Whipsnade tree cathedral, where people sit when a service is held there. What do you think it feels like in this cathedral?*

Mr Blyth went on to create the Whipsnade tree cathedral (right), by planting trees and avenues of grass in the layout of a great cathedral building.

Virtual visits

Many cathedral websites have 'virtual tours' and activities for children. Choose one to visit from www.englishcathedrals.co.uk. Which arts do people take part in there?

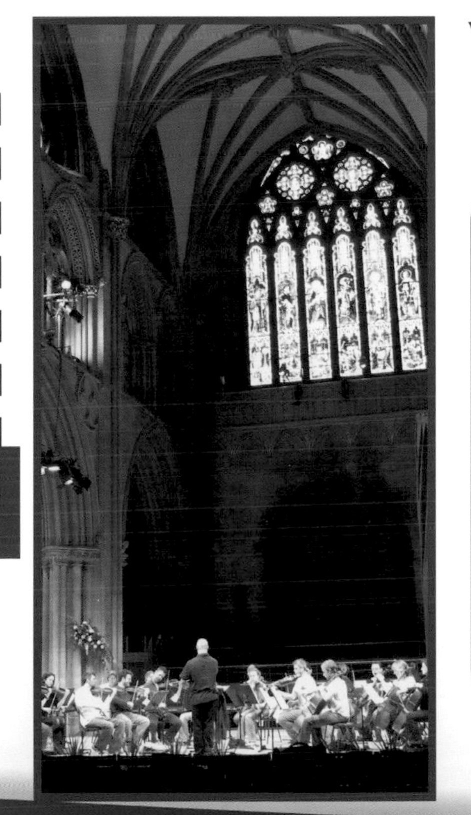

▶ *Why do you think classical music concerts often take place in cathedrals?*

▼ *After a visit to a cathedral, you could write a poem, like Chloe's about the Anglican cathedral in Liverpool.*

SPACE

Inside this stone building
Is .... space.
The candles shine like stars
And the brass glows gold like the sun.
Over there the font zooms upwards
Like a space shuttle.
Lamps glisten like moons
In this strange stone space.

(Chloe Lavery)

Stained-glass windows

If you ask people what makes churches different from other types of building, they often mention stained-glass windows. Light from outside shines through the coloured glass, to show the pictures, patterns and writing in the windows. Sometimes the light passing through the windows sends shafts of coloured light into the church.

Some of the oldest stained-glass windows were made in the 12th and 13th centuries, but people still design and make windows today. People also use their skills to restore and conserve older windows.

This window shows the story of Jesus turning water into wine (John 2: 3-11). Jesus and his mother are both shown with a halo, a symbol used in art to show a holy person. As in Christian holy books (see page 10), pictures of people are accepted in many churches.

Why were the windows made?

Many of the pictures in the windows show Bible stories and scenes from the lives of Christian saints. In medieval times, when very few people learned to read, the pictures were used to teach people who came to the church about the Bible and Christian beliefs. Today most people can read the Bible to find out about the stories, but often people say that a picture in a stained-glass window helps them to understand a story and makes it more meaningful.

The windows also beautify the church. Some windows are made in memory

The Bible in art

In a church or cathedral, find pictures of Bible stories – for example, in windows, paintings, wood carvings, stone carvings and on banners. Which do you like, and why?

This window illustrates a parable that Jesus told about a man who was attacked and robbed. Do you know what happens in the story, and who the man in the centre is? (See Luke 10: 25-37.)

of a person who used to worship at the church. The window is like a special 'thank-you gift', showing how much the person cared about the church.

The importance of light

In Christian belief, God is associated with light. In the Bible story of 'The Beginning' (Genesis 1: 3), God creates light on the first day. In the New Testament, when God sends his son Jesus to live in the world, Jesus is called 'the light of the world'. The way that light brings to life the pictures in a stained-glass window is sometimes likened to the idea of God's light coming in to a dark world.

Amy's class made stained-glass windows, from tissue paper, to illustrate the Resurrection, when Jesus is believed to have risen from death.

I like the way the light shines through stained-glass windows. They make me feel happy and relaxed.

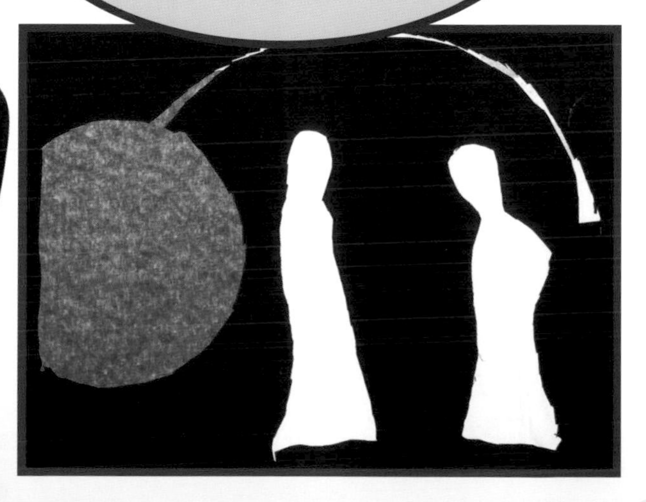

Different colours, different feelings

Colours of the rainbow

Think of the colours of the rainbow. Which colours would you choose to express happiness, calm, and strength? Ask some other people and see if they choose the same colours as you to express these feelings.

Rainbow poem

Write a poem inspired by a rainbow, with a reference to each colour (red, orange, yellow, green, blue, indigo, violet) and what it means to you.

In science, have you learnt how a beam of light splits into rainbow colours when it is refracted, as it passes from one substance to another? This shows that normal 'white' light is, in fact, made up of all the other colours.

Because of this, the idea or image of a rainbow is sometimes used to express a belief that different things or different people are all part of one whole; the differences are needed, and make something beautiful.

▶ *Do you know how a rainbow is part of the Bible story of Noah? (Read Genesis 8 and 9, up to verse 17.)*

▼ *In some churches, beautiful cloths are made to cover the altar. The altar is where bread and wine are prepared for communion, when Christians remember the Last Supper that Jesus took with his disciples before his crucifixion. What feelings do you think this rainbow altar cloth gives to people?*

Colours through the year

In some churches, different-coloured altar cloths are used for different festivals and times of year, as shown in the chart below.
At services, the church leaders also wear vestments of these different colours.

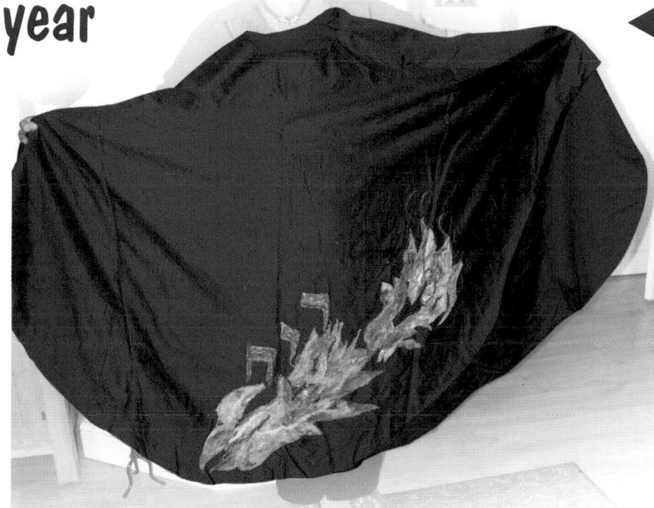

This robe was made for a Roman Catholic priest, for the service when he was first made a priest. Red, for fire, is a reminder of the Bible story of Pentecost (Acts 2), when God's spirit appeared like flames, inspiring Jesus's disciples and giving them courage to tell other people about Jesus.

Colour	Examples of when it is used	Meanings
White	Christmas Day, Easter Day, All Saints Day, Weddings	Light, innocence, purity, joy, glory
Red	Holy Week (except Maundy Thursday), Pentecost, Festivals of saints who were martyrs	Fire, blood, God's love, sacrifice
Purple	Advent, Lent (up to Holy Week)	Gloom, penitence, humility, quietness
Green	Most ordinary times, between the special days already mentioned	Plants and trees, hope of eternal life, the Holy Ghost

These colours are used in many churches. In religions other than Christianity the colours may have different meanings.

Another place where colours have symbolic meanings is in paintings called icons (see more on page 19). In this icon of Jesus as a child, with his mother Mary, gold represents God's light shining everywhere.

Picturing Jesus

Jesus lived about 2,000 years ago in the land that is now Israel. Christians call him the Son of God. They believe that, in Jesus, God became a human being and experienced life in the way that all people do. They say that, in a mysterious way, Jesus was both completely human and completely divine.

How is he pictured?

In the Bible, the gospels tell what Jesus did and said, what he was like, and the effect he had on people. They do not say what he looked like. Jesus was Jewish and so, in making pictures of him, some artists try to imagine how a 1st-century Jewish man, born in the Middle East, would have looked. However, many artists portray Jesus as if he is in their own time and place, and so there are different styles of pictures of Jesus from different countries and from different times in history.

▶ *This South African sculpture of Jesus represents his saying, 'I am the good shepherd' (John 10: 11).*

▲ *Many pictures of Jesus show events in his life, such as his birth, his baptism, the Last Supper and his crucifixion. What feelings are there in this 16th-century painting by the Italian artist Pordenone, as Jesus carries the cross on which he will be crucified?*

People may make Jesus look like themselves because it is easier to paint or sculpt what they are familiar with, but it also means that they relate to Jesus as someone like them, and feel closer to him. In their pictures of Jesus, artists often express what they believe and feel about him.

Picture gallery

Find as many pictures of Jesus as you can, choose your favourite three and think what they tell you about Jesus and about the artist. What does your choice say about you? One website to try is www.rejesus.co.uk/expressions/faces_jesus.

In 2000, the people of Whalton, Northumberland, all took photographs for an exhibition of what their village means to them. Copies of the photographs were made, and artist Ian Johnson put together sections of nearly 3,000 of them to make this picture of the 'Whalton Christ'. It expresses the belief that Jesus still lives among people today.

Icons

A way of painting stylised pictures called icons, of Jesus and other holy people, developed in Orthodox Christianity. The main purpose of icons is to help people pray. They are often called 'windows' between people and God, so, by meditating on an icon, a person feels closer to God.

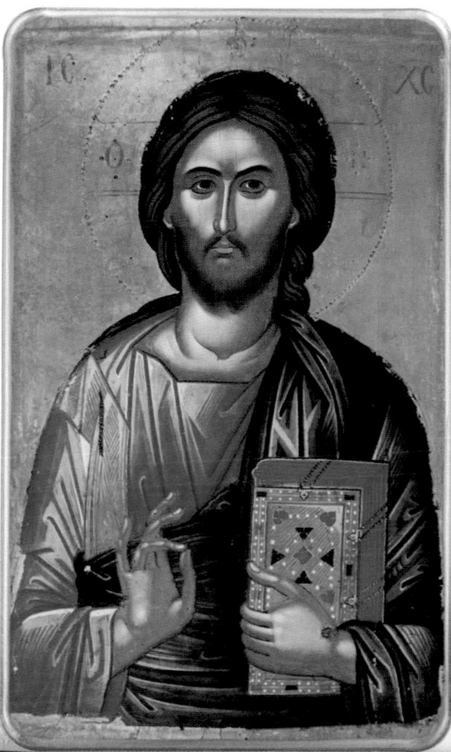

Icon artists follow rules about colours, shapes and symbols. For example, they always show both eyes and at least one ear of the holy person. For more about icons, go to www.juniors.reonline.org.uk and find the virtual tour of Greek Orthodox Christianity.

This icon shows Jesus Christ as ruler of the universe. His blue and red robes symbolise his divine and human nature. He holds a book, a sign of a teacher.

Islamic art

Muslims believe that they should not make any images of people or living creatures. Instead, they have developed styles of art that feature patterns and calligraphy. Many mosques are decorated with patterns, which are sometimes made with coloured mosaic tiles. The same types of patterns are made around the text in some special Qur'ans (see page 10).

A mosque may have a pattern like this in the domed ceiling. What feeling do you think it gives inside the building?

Islamic patterns are usually tessellating, which means that they have repeating shapes that fit together. The painting below right is by Zarah Hussain. She explains that the patterns can be created by dividing up circles in clever ways, and that there are religious reasons for using the patterns. She says:

The circle has no beginning and no end and that is a metaphor for the divine – it's never-ending.

This painting is by Zarah Hussain, a modern Muslim artist who has studied Islamic art and learnt how to make the geometric patterns.

Do some Islamic art

Download some Islamic calligraphy, tiles or patterns to colour in, from www.geocities.com/mutmainaa/kids/

Arabic calligraphy

Another way in which Muslims make beautiful artistic decoration is to use the skilful writing of the Arabic language. Arabic is written from right to left, in graceful, sweeping shapes which can be formed into calligraphy. Verses from the Qur'an, sayings of the Prophet Muhammad, and other religious texts are used to decorate the walls of mosques and Muslim homes. They can look beautiful as well as remind Muslims of their teaching. Trained calligraphers work in distinctive styles, with care, devotion and skill.

▼ *Panels of embroidered calligraphy are made each year to hang around the holy building called the Ka'bah in Makkah. After the time of the Hajj, the annual Muslim pilgrimage to Makkah, sections of the embroidered panels are given to people, who treasure them greatly.*

Prayer mats

In desert countries where Islam began, wood was not easily available and cushions and rugs were often used as furniture. These are often richly coloured and patterned. The prayer mats that Muslims use to perform their five daily prayers are made in traditional styles, and some have pictures of the holy mosques at Makkah, Madinah and Jerusalem.

▶ *Muslims use a prayer mat as a 'portable mosque'. It can be put down wherever they are, making a clean place to pray. Many mats have an arch design which can be placed to point towards Makkah, the direction in which Muslims face to pray.*

Drama and plays telling Christian stories

What differences are there between:

- reading a story
- seeing the story presented as a play or film
- taking part in a drama or play of the story?

When you watch a drama of a story, it's interesting if you can 'freeze' the action at times, to think about what the different characters are thinking and feeling. You could try this with one of the pictures here.

At Christmas, in some churches, people put on Nativity plays, acting the story of when Jesus was born, as it is told in the gospels.

It's moving, imagining being Mary, the mother of Jesus. It helps me to think how normal and yet how special the baby Jesus was.

Using drama at church services

At some churches, in some of the services, a group of people from the church act a Bible story, or a scene based on a Christian teaching. They may use their imaginations to present a Bible story as it would happen in today's world, with modern characters. The drama can help the actors and the people who watch to think about the story and what it means. It can bring the story to life and show its importance.

Act a parable

In a group, work out how you could act the parable of the lost son (Luke 15: 11-32). Try to set the story in your town today.

performance-places around the town. The guilds were called ‘mysteries’ and so the plays became known as ‘mystery plays’.

In the 16th century, after the Reformation, the plays were banned, but some of them have now been revived, for example in York. You can find out more at www.yorkmysteryplays.org.

In the 2002 York mystery plays, the group on this wagon presented the story of Moses in Egypt.

Mystery plays

In medieval times, in York, Chester, Coventry and other towns around the UK, people put on plays showing episodes from the Bible, from the story of God creating the world to Jesus’s death and resurrection and the time when Christians believe that Jesus will come to earth again, called ‘the Last Judgement’. Each episode was presented on its own wagon, by a different guild of craftsmen (for example, the shipbuilders’ guild performed the story of Noah’s Ark), and the wagons were pulled to

Passion plays

In several towns today, Christians get together to put on plays at Easter, acting out events from Jesus’s life, his death on the cross, and the times when his followers saw him again after his resurrection. The plays are sometimes called Passion plays. Presented in open, public places, they are a way to tell people about Jesus. They also help people to think about Jesus being part of their lives today.

In this scene from an Easter play presented in Edinburgh, Jesus heals a blind person. What would you feel if you were an onlooker?

Hindu art, dance and drama

Hindu art, dance and drama are usually based on ancient stories of gods and goddesses. Many Hindus say that all these deities are really different aspects of one ultimate being, or god, who is too complicated to be fully understood or represented.

Pictures of the deities

Statues and pictures of Hindu deities include details from stories about them and symbols of their powers and tasks.

Looking at the pictures, Hindus often meditate on the qualities of the deity – for instance, the courage and devotion of the monkey god Hanuman, from the story of Rama and Sita – and this helps them to follow the deity's example.

One special type of Hindu art is floor-painting of patterns, called rangoli in North India and kolam in South India. The most common designs start with dots, which are connected to make lines and shapes. More elaborate patterns are made at Divali time. A Hindu woman explains:

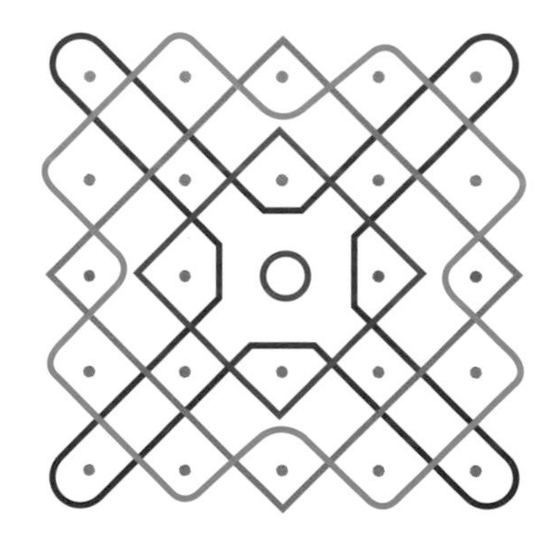

The dots stand for hurdles and problems in life. Our life begins from the Lord, runs around various hurdles, and finally ends again with the Lord.

This statue shows the god Shiva as 'Lord of the Dance'. He is doing the dance of destruction to make way for the creation of a new universe. He has four arms. In one hand he holds a drum to make the rhythm of the dance of creation, in another a bowl of the fire of destruction. One hand is held out in blessing and one points to his dancing feet, which trample on the demon of ignorance, as he juggles the ring of fire. Shiva is especially honoured by Hindu dancers.

Dance and drama

Hindu dance and drama are considered to be forms of worship and meditation. Different types of traditional dance began in temples in different areas of India. The dances tell stories from the Hindu scriptures, such as the stories of Rama and Sita, and Krishna and Radha, the milkmaid.

The dances are very skilful and hard to learn, involving an elaborate system of postures, gestures and foot movements. In one style, there are 13 postures of the head, 9 of the neck, 36 of the eye, and 37 of the hand.

In Hindu dances, head and hand movements are used to tell stories of the deities. This man is being Shiva, holding a deer.

This woman is showing a goddess who is asleep and having sweet dreams.

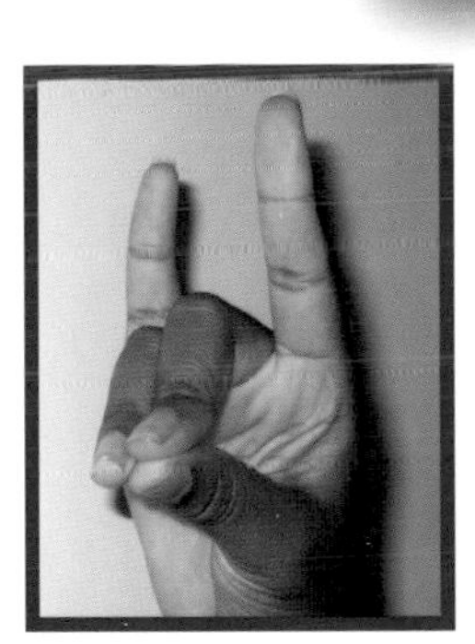

Try making your hand this shape and moving it to represent a deer leaping along in the forest, in the Rama and Sita story.

Puppet shows are also a traditional way of performing Hindu stories. Stick puppets, like this one of Rama, from Indonesia, were used to give shadow puppet shows.

Costumes and make-up for a type of dance called Kathakali make the characters look magical and 'from another world'.

Puppet story

Choose a short story to present in a shadow puppet show. Make puppets from cut-out paper figures fixed to straws, and use an overhead projector to show them as you retell the story.

Present a story through drama

You could combine your RE work with your work in drama, as shown here. The children found out about the symbols used in pictures of the Hindu god Ganesh, and presented their findings in a series of 'freeze frames'. They wrote a script for two narrators, prepared simple costumes and props, and worked hard to show the feelings of all the characters. Which religious story could you present in this way?

Pictures of Ganesh show him with an elephant's head on a fat human body, a broken tusk, a bowl of sweets, a rat, and a belt made from a snake. Find out why, from the children's drama.

Spot the feelings

Study the freeze frames of the Ganesh story on these two pages. What feelings are the different characters showing in their expressions and body language?

The narrators' script

Ganesh was a special boy. His mum, the goddess Parvati, had made him with her special powers. She asked him to stand guard outside their home, while she took a bath.

Parvati's husband, the god Shiva, returned and Ganesh would not let him in. Shiva was so filled with rage that he took out his sword and chopped off Ganesh's head.

Parvati was horrified and heart-broken. She pleaded with Shiva to bring Ganesh back.

Shiva sent his soldiers to find another head. The first animal they found was an elephant. They zapped it and took its head for Ganesh.

Parvati and Shiva loved Ganesh and spoiled him. They gave him sweets whenever he wanted, and soon he became very fat!

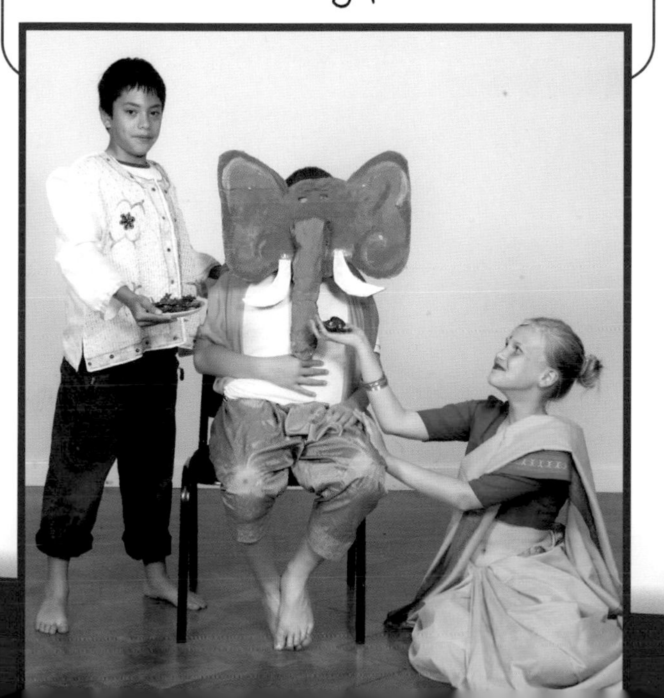

Ganesh had a rat to ride on. He went to a party and, as usual, ate too many sweets. He felt so full that he had to really concentrate on not falling off his rat. Lurking by the road was a snake. It hissed at the rat and Ganesh fell off. His tummy burst open and all his sweets fell out!

Ganesh tried to stuff the sweets back into his tummy, and used the snake as a belt. He did look funny, but he was offended when he heard someone laughing at him. Who? He looked up and saw it was the moon! In anger, Ganesh broke off one of his tusks and threw it at the moon.

Glossary

Anglican belonging to the Church of England.

artefact an object (for example, a dish, a candle, a cushion) made with human skill.

baptism a religious ceremony involving immersion in, or pouring or sprinkling of, water. Jesus was baptised by John the Baptist in the River Jordan.

calligrapher an artist who produces beautiful writing (calligraphy), with a pen or paintbrush.

cathedral a large important church that contains a bishop's throne (the 'cathedra').

chant to recite words in a singing, rhythmic way; in a type of church music, to sing prose.

Christ a title given to Jesus, meaning the expected Messiah sent by God.

commandment in the Bible, a law for God's people, given by God to Moses.

communion a Christian service using bread and wine which recalls the last meal of Jesus and celebrates his sacrificial death and resurrection. It is also called Holy Communion, Eucharist, Mass or the Lord's Supper.

crucifixion being put to death on a cross, a punishment used in Roman times.

deity a god or goddess.

devotion deep love and spiritual feeling.

Divali the Hindu festival of light, remembering the happy ending of the story of Rama and Sita.

divine of or from God.

gospel a book of the Christian Bible telling the life of Jesus. There are four gospels.

gurdwara a Sikh place of worship or temple.

Hajj the pilgrimage to Makkah, which Muslims should try to do once in their life.

halo a ring of light around the head of an angel or holy person in religious art.

harmonium a musical instrument where air is squeezed through reeds to make the sound while a tune is played on the keyboard.

hymn a song of praise to God.

icon a painted image or mosaic of a holy person, believed itself to be holy, and used as an aid to worship, usually in the Orthodox branch of Christianity.

inspire to stimulate somebody to do something, especially to make art; to encourage someone to greater enthusiasm or creativity.

Ka'bah the cube-shaped shrine at the centre of the Grand Mosque in Makkah.

kolam the South Indian word for rangoli patterns.

Last Supper the last meal that Jesus ate with his disciples before his crucifixion.

mantle in a synagogue, a cover, like a cloak, for a Torah scroll.

Mass the term used in Roman Catholic and some other churches for the Eucharist, or communion.

monk a man who is a member of a religious community devoted to prayer.

mosque a Muslim place of worship.

Nativity the birth of Jesus, celebrated by Christians at Christmas.

nave the main part of a church, where the congregation sits.

New Testament the second part of the Christian Bible, starting with the gospels.

organ a musical instrument, traditional in churches. It is a wind instrument, with large pipes, a keyboard and pedals. Modern electronic organs are used in some churches today.

Orthodox the Eastern branch of Christianity.

parable a story that shows a moral truth.

Passion the sufferings of Jesus, especially in the time leading up to his crucifixion.

Pentecost the name of a Jewish festival when, according to the Christian Bible, the Holy Spirit came to Jesus's followers.

Qur'an the Muslim holy book, sometimes spelt 'Koran'.

ragees Sikh musicians who sing hymns, or ragas, from the Guru Granth Sahib.

rangoli traditional Hindu patterns made on the floor with coloured powder.

reconciliation the ending of conflict or renewing of a friendly relationship between disputing people or groups; 'making up' after a fight.

Reformation a 16th-century reform movement which led to the formation of Protestant Churches. It emphasised the need to return to the beliefs and practices of the early Church.

Resurrection the rising from the dead of Jesus on the third day after his crucifixion.

reverence a feeling of deep love and respect.

Roman Catholic Christian denomination that regards the Pope as head of the Church.

saint a particularly good or holy person, usually believed to have gone to heaven after death.

service a ceremony or meeting for worship, usually involving set words and prayers.

stylised made into an artistic image rather than a realistic picture.

tabla an Indian musical instrument consisting of a pair of small drums played with the hands.

text a short passage from the Bible, displayed in some way or used as the subject for a religious talk.

Torah the main Jewish holy book consisting of the first five books of the Bible. Handwritten scrolls of the Torah are the most precious items in a synagogue.

traditional based on valued customs which have been handed down from generation to generation.

unison sounding absolutely together.

Vespers an evening church service.

vestments robes worn by leaders during a religious ceremony.

For teachers and parents

This book has been designed to support and extend the learning objectives of Unit 6F of the QCA Religious Education Scheme of Work, 'How do people express their faith through the arts?' It provides thought-provoking examples from several major religions to enable children to explore the creativity and spirituality involved in the expression of religious feelings, beliefs and ideas. It contributes to the 'appreciation and wonder' aspect of RE, as identified in the Non-Statutory Framework for RE, helping children to develop imagination and wonder, recognise that knowledge is bounded by mystery, appreciate the sense of wonder and develop their capacity to respond to questions of meaning and purpose.

The content and suggested activities aim to help children to learn both 'about religion' (AT1) and 'from religion' (AT2), as identified in the Non-Statutory Framework KS2 1e, 3i, and especially to provide opportunities for 'expressing and communicating their own and others' insights' through art and design, music, dance, drama and ICT (3r). Links are made between RE and the expressive arts areas of the curriculum, and examples of art, poetry and drama by KS2 children are shown.

FURTHER INFORMATION AND ACTIVITIES

Pages 4-5 How do people express their feelings?
This is an opportunity to draw together and review creative aspects of the curriculum the class has been covering in music, art, drama, dance, and creative writing, and to relate these to expressing feelings.

'Joy' was written by a nine-year-old for an anthology of children's poetry about feelings. Your class could produce a similar anthology over a period.

Pages 6-7 Think about being creative
Link to D&T, 'designing and making assignments using a range of materials', giving the children an opportunity to create something out of the natural shapes of stones or other items.

The creation story in Genesis is used as inspiration for poetry in Sandy Brownjohn's book, *The Ability to Name Cats*, and this could provide a useful way to link children's creativity to the idea of God creating the world. (All Sandy Brownjohn's books on teaching children to write poetry are full of inspirational ideas.)

Discuss the children's own feeling of achievement about having created something in poetry, art, music, D&T, and whether they think creativity is what makes human beings spiritual.

The Reconciliation sculpture is emotionally powerful. (This one is in the ruined part of Coventry Cathedral and an identical one, with the same explanation on its plaque, in English and Japanese, is in Hiroshima.) To help children to 'feel' it, they could explore their own experiences of 'making up' after a broken friendship or read moving examples of forgiveness at www.theforgivenessproject.com or in stories, as well as linking to the historical context.

Pages 8-9 How do people use music in worship?
Try Beethoven's 'Ode to Joy', or 'Happy we' from Handel's *Acis and Galatea,* as music expressing joy. Link to the Music NC by arranging for children to listen to 'a range of live and recorded music from different times and cultures' with audio or video recordings of music from various faiths, and various styles within Christian music.

Let children write 'reviews' for a class magazine or webpage, including describing the emotions they felt when listening.

Invite a musician to sing/play and be interviewed about why they do it and how they feel using their music in worship.

Think about why Muslims do not use music in worship, and listen to the chant of a muezzin or a reading from the Qur'an at www.islamicity.com or http://quranexplorer.com.

Pages 10-11 Creating beautiful books and texts
The British Library's online resource 'Turning the pages' enables you to look at pages of manuscripts including a Qur'an, a Hebrew Bible, the Lindisfarne Gospels and other famous sacred texts. Go to www.bl.uk>online gallery>turning the pages.

See www.museumofpsalms.com/psalms.php for a Jewish artist's paintings (with no people depicted) of the 150 psalms in the Bible.

Robert Cooper is a photographer and calligrapher interested in the link between creativity and spirituality. See http://cooperphoto.co.uk.

Children can use ICT graphic packages to experiment with calligraphy, at the simplest to make a large hollow capital letter or first word of a text to decorate like an 'illuminated' manuscript.

They could design and make a gift of a beautiful bookmark with an appropriate short text.

Pages 12-13 Cathedral building
There are links to some cathedral websites from http://juniors.reonline.org.uk and there are virtual tours of some cathedrals at http://www.request.org.uk/main/main.htm>churches> looking at church buildings.

Whipsnade tree cathedral is a National Trust property in Bedfordshire. Its section on the NT website gives its history and some teaching ideas.

Pages 14-15 Stained-glass windows
The Canterbury Cathedral website has useful information on stained-glass windows: www.canterbury-cathedral.org/index.htm.

Children can make 'stained-glass' pictures with black sugar paper and tissue paper or coloured cellophane. The designs need simple shapes.

Pages 16-17 Different colours, different feelings
Make a 'colourful' display of phrases using colour (eg 'green with envy'). Children could create their own by thinking how each colour makes them feel.

Group children according to their favourite colour, to make a collage of items of that colour cut from magazines and write a poem about it.

You could link with science by using prisms to split white light or, conversely, spinning a multi-coloured disc to make it look white.

Feelings about colour are subjective, but also cultural; for example, in Asian countries, white is the colour of death and brides wear red.

A local clergyman or woman might be willing, either at the church or at school, to 'dress up' in and explain his or her liturgical vestments.

Pages 18-19 Picturing Jesus
Contact the education officer at a local art gallery to arrange a visit focusing on the subject, if possible.

Margaret Cooling's books *Jesus through Art* and *The Bible through Art* (RMEP) include a variety of pictures and ideas for linking art to RE.

Further websites with pictures of Jesus are:
www.lostseed.com/extras/free-graphics/jesus-pictures.php
www.religionfacts.com/jesus/image_gallery.htm

An icon painter Vasiliki Papantoniou explains
the meaning of icons at

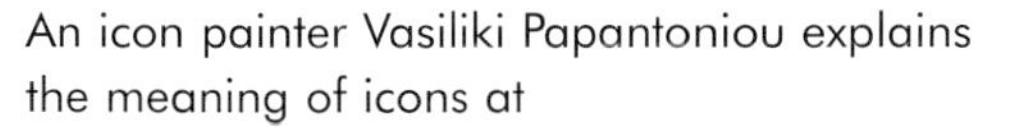

www.travelwithachallenge.com/Greek_Islands_Icon_Artist.htm.
www.ocf.org/OrthodoxPage/icons/icons.html has icons and clipart icons which can be downloaded.

To look more generally at 'religious art', go to www.bbc.co.uk/whereilive, choose an area of the country, and see whether, in the 'Faith' section, there is a section of 'divine art'.

Pages 20-21 Islamic art
Muslim attitudes to depictions of Muhammad are discussed on http://en.wikipedia.org/wiki/Depictions_of_Muhammad and www.pbs.org/empires/islam/cultureart.html.

Visit the Islamic gallery at the Victoria and Albert Museum: www.vam.ac.uk/collections/asia/islamic_gall. (Go to 'style in Islamic art' or 'videos: Islamic architecture'.)

http://haqaonline.lightuponlight.com/pg/ has pictures of mosques.

See more work by Zarah Hussain at www.zarahhussain.co.uk.

Children could paint 'calligraphy' or graffiti 'tag' of their own names.

Pages 22-23 Drama and plays telling Christian stories
A 'Life of Christ' play and Nativity plays are put on at the Wintershall Estate. See www.wintershall-estate.com.

Children could write a story or poem about being a character in a Nativity play. They could ask their parents if they remember seeing them in a school Nativity play, and how it felt. Read the two accounts, in Matthew and Luke, which are usually 'conflated', edited and embellished, and discuss what is done to turn the accounts into drama.

Pages 24-25 Hindu art, dance and drama
www.geocities.com/Athens/Acropolis/1863/kolam.html has fun kolam drawing tools and generator pages, and links to kolam tutorials.

www.lotussculpture.com/nataraja1.htm shows a dancing Shiva in detail.

www.re-net.ac.uk >Hinduism>hindu deities has notes for teachers about iconography and www.hindunet.org/hindu has pictures of gods and goddesses. Select some and help children to 'de-code' them by relating details to stories, as is done for Ganesh on pages 26-27.

http://hinduism.about.com/od/dancesofindia/Dances_of_India.htm has a 'brief introduction to dances of India'.

Groups of children could work out how to 'tell' a favourite story through a dance with gestures, telling the story and explaining the gestures to the class before, or after, a performance.

For the Rama and Sita story, see the book in this series on *How and why do Hindus and Sikhs celebrate Divali?*

Pages 26-27 Present a story through drama
The Ganesh story was chosen here as a variation from the usual, well-known Rama and Sita story. For pictures and stories of Ganesh, see http://hinduism.about.com/od/lordganesha/ Lord_Ganesha.htm.

In choosing a story to dramatise, be aware that this approach is not acceptable for Muslim stories.

Photographs and narration from a freeze-frame presentation can be made into a display, IWB resource or book.

USEFUL WEBSITES

www.qca.org.uk >I am interested in>Subjects>Religious Education> Useful resources

Spirited Arts is a National Association of Teachers of RE (NATRE) project to link creativity with Religious Education for schools. See www.natre.org.uk/spiritedarts for poetry and art galleries of examples of children's work and annual competitions you might like to enter.

www.reonline.org.uk is a 'gateway' RE site and has a child-friendly junior section, including virtual visits to places of worship.

www.request.org.uk is an excellent site for a wide range of work on Christianity and links to different types of churches.

www.re-xs.ucsm.ac.uk is another useful gateway site.

Adam 7
altar cloths 16, 17

Bible 8, 10, 15, 18
stories 14, 15, 16, 17, 22, 23
Blyth, E. K. 13
body language 4, 26

calligraphers and calligraphy 10, 11, 20, 21
cathedrals 9, 12-13
Lichfield 12
Liverpool 13
St Albans 12
Westminster 9
Whipsnade tree cathedral 13
chanting 9
choirs 9
Christians 8, 10, 11, 14, 15, 16-17, 22, 23
Christmas 17, 22
churches 8, 9, 14, 15, 16, 22
colours 14, 16, 17, 19
Cooper, Robert 11
creativity 7

dance 24, 25
drama 4, 22-23, 25, 26-27

Easter 17, 23
eyes 4, 19, 25

facial expressions 4
festivals 9, 16, 17

Ganesh 5, 26, 27
God 7, 10, 12
as creator 7, 15, 23
in Christian belief 15, 17, 18
praising God 8, 9
gurdwara 8
Guru Granth Sahib 8

halo 14
harmonium 8
Hindu art 5, 24
Hindu dance and drama 24, 25
holy books 8, 10, 11
(*see also* Bible, Guru Granth Sahib, Qur'an, Torah)
Hussain, Zarah 20
hymns 8

icons 17, 19
Islamic art 20-21

Jesus 11, 14, 15, 16, 17, 18, 19, 22, 23
Jews 10, 11, 14
Johnson, Ian 19

light 14, 15, 16, 17, 19

Michelangelo 7
mosques 20, 21
music 5, 8-9, 13
Muslims 9, 10, 20, 21
mystery plays 23

Nativity plays 22

organ 9

parables 15, 22
Passion plays 23
patterns 10, 14, 20, 24
Pentecost 17
pictures 5, 6, 10, 12, 14, 15
in holy books 10, 14
of Hindu deities 5, 24, 26
of Jesus 14, 17, 18, 19
poems 5
postures 4, 25
prayer mats 21
prayers and praying 8, 9, 11, 21
puppets 25

Qur'an 10, 20, 21

ragees 8
rainbow 16
Rama and Sita 24, 25
rangoli patterns 24
Reconciliation (sculpture) 7
Resurrection 15, 23

sculpture 7, 18
Shiva 24, 26, 27
Sikhs 8
singing 5, 8, 9

tabla 8
texts 11, 21
Torah 11

vestments 17

Whalton Christ 19
windows, stained-glass 12, 14-15

Young, Lana 11